Using Simple Machines

Pulleys All Around

by Trudy Becker

FOCUS READERS

PIONEER

www.focusreaders.com

Copyright © 2024 by Focus Readers®, Lake Elmo, MN 55042. All rights reserved. No part of this book may be reproduced or utilized in any form or by any means without written permission from the publisher.

Focus Readers is distributed by North Star Editions:
sales@northstareditions.com | 888-417-0195

Produced for Focus Readers by Red Line Editorial.

Photographs ©: Shutterstock Images, cover, 1, 4, 6, 10, 12; iStockphoto, 8, 14, 17, 18, 20

Library of Congress Cataloging-in-Publication Data
Names: Becker, Trudy, author.
Title: Pulleys all around / by Trudy Becker.
Description: Lake Elmo, MN : Focus Readers, [2024] | Series: Using simple machines | Includes bibliographical references and index. | Audience: Grades K-1
Identifiers: LCCN 2022059238 (print) | LCCN 2022059239 (ebook) | ISBN 9781637395998 (hardcover) | ISBN 9781637396568 (paperback) | ISBN 9781637397688 (ebook pdf) | ISBN 9781637397138 (hosted ebook)
Subjects: LCSH: Pulleys--Juvenile literature.
Classification: LCC TJ1103 .B43 2024 (print) | LCC TJ1103 (ebook) | DDC 621.8--dc23/eng/20230103
LC record available at https://lccn.loc.gov/2022059238
LC ebook record available at https://lccn.loc.gov/2022059239

Printed in the United States of America
Mankato, MN
082023

About the Author

Trudy Becker lives in Minneapolis, Minnesota. She likes exploring new places and loves anything involving books.

Table of Contents

CHAPTER 1
Up and In 5

CHAPTER 2
What Are Pulleys? 9

CHAPTER 3
Pulleys Everywhere 13

THAT'S AMAZING!
Well Water 16

CHAPTER 4
Fun with Pulleys 19

Focus on Pulleys • 22
Glossary • 23
To Learn More • 24
Index • 24

Chapter 1

Up and In

A family buys a table. It's too big to go up the stairs. But it can fit through the window. So, the movers set up a machine. They pull the table into the air. Then they bring it inside.

The movers' machine uses a pulley. It has a rope and a wheel. Those parts help lift things upward. Pulleys are one of the six **simple machines**.

Fun Fact Pulleys can move things side to side, too.

Chapter 2

What Are Pulleys?

All simple machines help people do jobs. A pulley can help people lift a **load**. The load is attached to one side of a rope or **cable**. People can lift the load more easily by pulling.

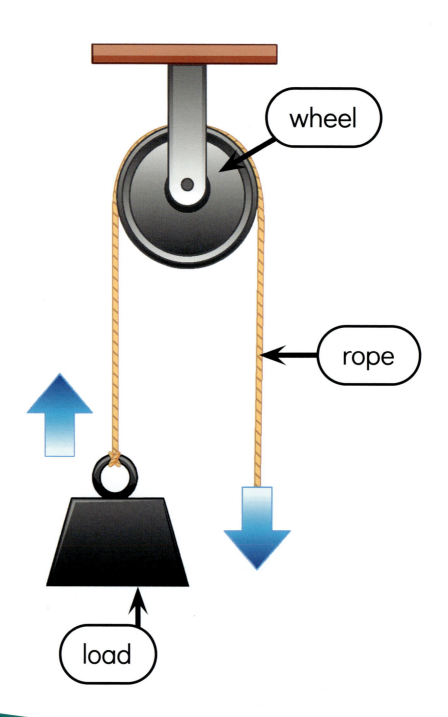

A pulley has two parts. There is a rope or cable. There is a wheel, too. The wheel has a **groove** to fit the rope. When the rope is pulled, the wheel turns. The load moves up.

Fun Fact

Simple pulleys are machines with one pulley. **Compound** pulleys have more than one.

Chapter 3

Pulleys Everywhere

Pulleys are all around. Builders lift things up with pulleys. Elevators use pulleys to move up and down. Flagpoles use pulleys, too.

Sometimes pulleys help bring things down. Ships put down lifeboats with pulleys. Those pulleys use a **block and tackle**. That helps when loads are very heavy.

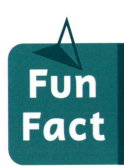

Fun Fact Many window blinds use pulleys to open.

That's Amazing!

Well Water

Some people get water with pulleys. They lower a bucket into a well. The bucket fills up. Then, they can **hoist** it out. They pull on the rope. The bucket rises. They could get water without the pulley. But it would take more **force**.

Chapter 4

Fun with Pulleys

Pulleys are used for hard jobs. But they can be used for fun, too. **Zip lines** use pulleys. Riders zoom fast. Rock climbers use pulleys to go up and down.

Sometimes people go sailing for fun. Sailboats have lots of pulleys. Sailors pull on ropes to raise the sails. They can move different parts around. Then the sails catch the wind.

Fun Fact People have used pulleys for thousands of years.

FOCUS ON
Pulleys

Write your answers on a separate piece of paper.

1. Write a sentence that explains the main idea of Chapter 2.

2. What is the most helpful way you use pulleys in your life? Why?

3. What part of a pulley helps the rope wrap around the wheel?
    - A. load
    - B. groove
    - C. machine

4. What is the difference between simple and compound pulleys?
    - A. the number of pulleys
    - B. the size of the pulleys
    - C. the weight of the pulleys

Answer key on page 24.

Glossary

block and tackle
A system with one pulley (or group of pulleys) that moves with the load and one pulley (or group) that doesn't.

cable
A rope made of wire.

compound
Made up of two or more parts.

force
A push or pull that changes how something moves.

groove
A long, hollow space cut into a surface.

hoist
To raise or lift something by pulling.

load
An object that is lifted or moved.

simple machines
Machines with only a few parts that make work easier.

zip lines
Pulley systems that let people slide along sloped cables.

To Learn More

BOOKS

Blevins, Wiley. *Let's Find Pulleys*. North Mankato, MN: Capstone Press, 2021.

Mattern, Joanne. *Pulleys*. Minneapolis: Bellwether Media, 2020.

NOTE TO EDUCATORS

Visit **www.focusreaders.com** to find lesson plans, activities, links, and other resources related to this title.

Index

C
compound pulleys, 11

G
groove, 11

H
hoisting, 16

S
sailing, 21

Answer Key: 1. Answers will vary; **2.** Answers will vary; **3.** B; **4.** A